CAMBRIDGE PRIMARY
Mathematics

Skills Builder

Name: _____

Contents

Cherri Moseley and Janet Rees

CAMBRIDGE
UNIVERSITY PRESS

University Printing House, Cambridge CB2 8BS, United Kingdom

One Liberty Plaza, 20th Floor, New York, NY 10006, USA

477 Williamstown Road, Port Melbourne, VIC 3207, Australia

314–321, 3rd Floor, Plot 3, Splendor Forum, Jasola District Centre, New Delhi – 110025, India

103 Penang Road, #05-06/07, Visioncrest Commercial, Singapore 238467

Cambridge University Press is part of the University of Cambridge.

It furthers the University's mission by disseminating knowledge in the pursuit of education, learning and research at the highest international levels of excellence.

www.cambridge.org
Information on this title: www.cambridge.org/9781316509135

First published 2016

20 19 18 17 16 15 14 13 12

Printed in Italy by Rotolito S.p.A.

A catalogue record for this publication is available from the British Library

ISBN 978-1-316-50913-5 Paperback

This book is part of the Cambridge Primary Maths project. This is an innovative combination of curriculum and resources designed to support teachers and learners to succeed in primary mathematics through best-practice international maths teaching and a problem-solving approach.

To get involved, visit
www.cie.org.uk/cambridgeprimarymaths.

Introduction

This *Skills Builder activity book* is part of a series of 12 write-in activity books for primary mathematics grades 1–6. It can be used as a standalone book, but the content also complements *Cambridge Primary Maths*. Learners progress at different rates, so this series provides a Skills Builder and a Challenge activity book for each Primary Mathematics Curriculum Framework Stage to support and broaden the depth of learning.

The *Skills Builder* books consolidate the learning already covered in the classroom, but provide extra support by giving short reminders of key information, topic vocabulary and hints on how best to develop maths skills and knowledge. They have also been written to support learners whose first language is not English.

How to use the books

The activities are for use by learners in school or at home, with adult mediation. Topics have been carefully chosen to focus on those common areas where learners might need extra support. The approach is linked directly to *Cambridge Primary Maths*, but teachers and parents can pick and choose which activities to cover, or go through the books in sequence.

The varied set of activities grow in challenge through each unit, including:

- closed questions with answers, so progress can be checked
- questions with more than one possible answer
- activities requiring resources, for example, dice, spinners or digit cards
- activities and games best done with someone else, for example, in class or at home, which give the opportunity to be fully involved in the child's learning
- activities to support different learning styles: working individually, in pairs, in groups.

How to approach the activities

Space is provided for learners to write their answers in the book. Some activities might need further practice or writing, so students could be given a blank notebook at the start of the year to use alongside the book. Each activity follows a standard structure.

- **Remember** gives an overview of key learning points. They introduce core concepts and, later, can be used as a revision guide. These sections should be read with an adult who can check understanding before attempting the activities.
- **Vocabulary** assists with difficult mathematical terms, particularly when English is not the learner's first language. Learners should read through the key vocabulary with an adult and be encouraged to clarify understanding.

- **Hints** prompt and assist in building understanding, and steer the learner in the right direction.
- **You will need** gives teachers and parents a list of resources for each activity.
- **Photocopiable resources** are provided at the end of the book, for easy assembly in class or at home.
- **Links** to the Cambridge International Examinations Primary Mathematics Curriculum Framework objectives and the corresponding *Cambridge Primary Mathematics Teacher's Resource* are given in the footnote on every page.
- **Calculators** should be used to help learners understand numbers and the number system, including place value and properties of numbers. However, the calculator is not promoted as a calculation tool before Stage 5.

Note:

When a 'spinner' is included, put a paperclip flat on the page so the end is over the centre of the spinner. Place the pencil point in the centre of the spinner, through the paperclip. Hold the pencil firmly and spin the paperclip to generate a result.

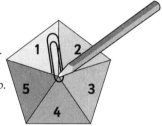

Tracking progress

Answers to closed questions are given at the back of the book; these allow teachers, parents and learners to check their work.

When completing each activity, teachers and parents are advised to encourage self-assessment by asking the students how straightforward they found the activity. When learners are reflecting on games, they should consider how challenging the mathematics was, not who won. Learners could use a ✓/ ✗ or red/green colouring system to record their self-assessment anywhere on each activity page.

These assessments provide teachers and parents with an understanding of how best to support individual learners' next steps.

Toy cupboard

Vocabulary
0, 1, 2, 3, 4, 5, 6, 7, 8, 9, 10, number, number pair

Remember
When you are counting, the numbers are always in the same order.

Hint: Touching each object in turn helps with counting.

Count. Write how many.

| 0 | 1 | 2 | 3 | 4 | 5 | 6 | 7 | 8 | 9 | 10 |

Unit 1A Number and problem solving
CPM Framework 1Nn1, 1Nn2, 1Nn3; CPM Teacher's Resource 1A: 1.1; 1.2

Make 10

You will need: counters in two different colours, matching colouring pencils

Use counters to make 10.

Make 10 in a different way each time.

Draw and colour your counters in the squares.

Vocabulary
count on, add, equals

Hint: 9 + 1 and 1 + 9 are two ways of making 10.

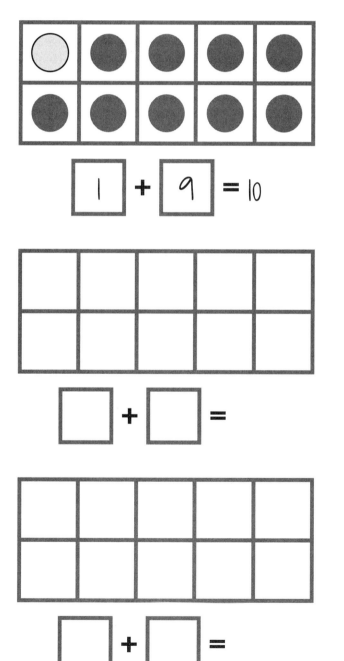

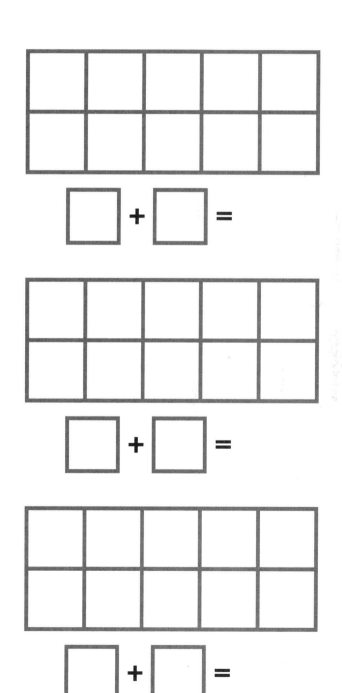

Dough worms

You will need: resource 1, page 52

Remember
Line up both objects so that they start from the same place.

Vocabulary
longer

shorter
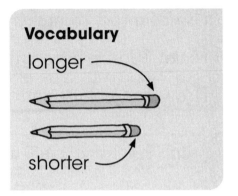

• Roll your dough into worms.

• Make a longer worm than this one.

• Draw around your worm.

• Make a shorter worm than this one.

• Draw around your worm.

• Compare your worms with a partner's worms.

Unit 1C Measure and problem solving
CPM Framework 1MI1, 1MI3; CPM Teacher's Resource 1C 3.1

Cube worms

Use five cubes to make a worm.

Find three things that are shorter than the cube worm.

Draw them.

You will need: five standard 2 centimetre cubes, joined together as a worm (or the worm cut from resource 2, page 53)

Vocabulary

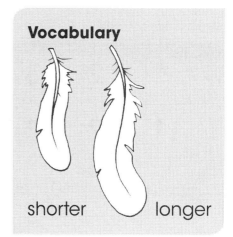

shorter   longer

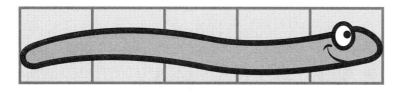

Find three things that are longer than the cube worm.

Draw them.

Numbers 11 to 20

Remember
When you are counting, the numbers are always in the same order.

Hint: Use place-value cards to help when writing numbers beyond 10.

1	2	3	4	5	6	7	8	9	10
11	12	13	14	15	16	17	18	19	20

Count on from 10. How many are there in each group?

10
1

10 and 1 makes [11]

10
2

10 and 2 makes [ ]

10
3

10 and [ ] makes [ ]

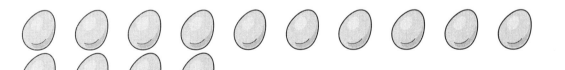

10
4

10 and [ ] makes [ ]

10
5

10 and ☐ makes ☐

10
6

10 and ☐ makes ☐

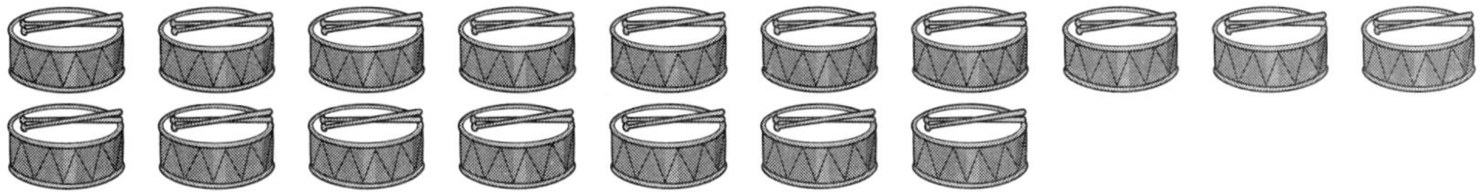

10
7

10 and ☐ makes ☐

10
8

10 and ☐ makes ☐

10
9

10 and ☐ makes ☐

10
10

10 and ☐ makes ☐

Estimating

Vocabulary

estimate, count, more, fewer

Remember

An estimate does not have to be the right answer.
It is a sensible guess.

Hint: Use a number track to help write the number.

Estimate how many   before you count.

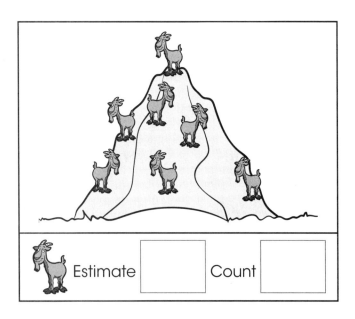

Estimate ☐ Count ☐

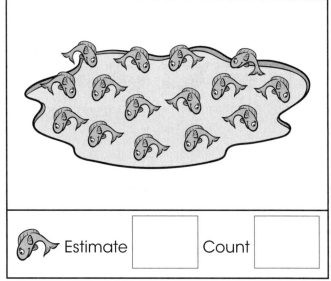

Estimate ☐ Count ☐

Estimate ☐ Count ☐

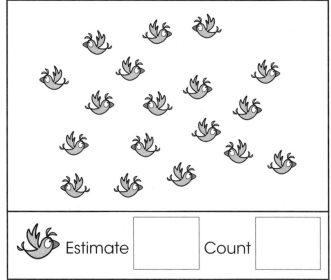

Estimate ☐ Count ☐

Estimate how many   .

Tick the box that matches your estimate.

Then count and write how many.

Hint: Use a number track to help decide which box to tick.

		Fewer than 10		More than 10	
		Count			
		Fewer than 10		More than 10	
		Count			
		Fewer than 10		More than 10	
		Count			
		Fewer than 10		More than 10	
		Count			
		Fewer than 10		More than 10	
		Count			

Unit 1A Number and problem solving
CPM Framework 1Nn1, 1Nn2, 1Nn3, 1Nn8, 1Pt2; CPM Teacher's Resource 5.1, 5.2

What's left?

Remember
2D shapes are flat.

Vocabulary
shape, flat, 2D, circle, triangle, square, rectangle, side, curved, straight

Hint: Resource 3, page 54, will help with the names of the shapes.

Tick (✓) each triangle.

Cross (✗) each square.

Colour each circle.

Which shape is left? _ e _ _ _ _ _ _ _

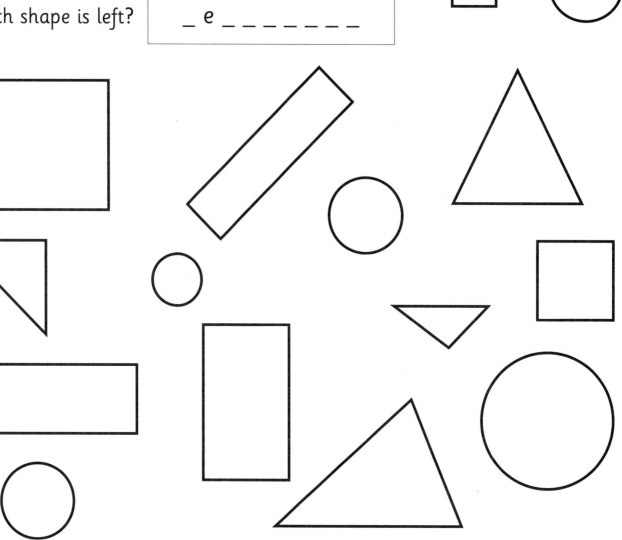

Tell a partner what you know about each shape.
How many sides does it have? Are they curved or straight?

Unit 1B Geometry and problem solving
CPM Framework 1Gs1; CPM Teacher's Resource 6.1

3D shape builder

Remember
3D shapes are solid.

Use 3D shapes to build a tower.

What else can you build?

Draw or take a picture of your model.

You will need: empty boxes and wooden blocks (cubes and cuboids), kitchen roll or crisp tubes, tins (cylinders), balls (spheres), other 3D shapes.

Vocabulary

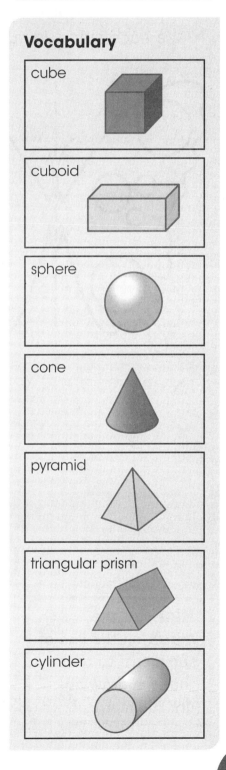

cube

cuboid

sphere

cone

pyramid

triangular prism

cylinder

Symmetry

You will need: a mirror

Remember

When a shape is symmetrical, each half is a mirror image of the other.

Vocabulary

symmetry   mirror line

line of symmetry

Complete each picture.
Make each side symmetrical.

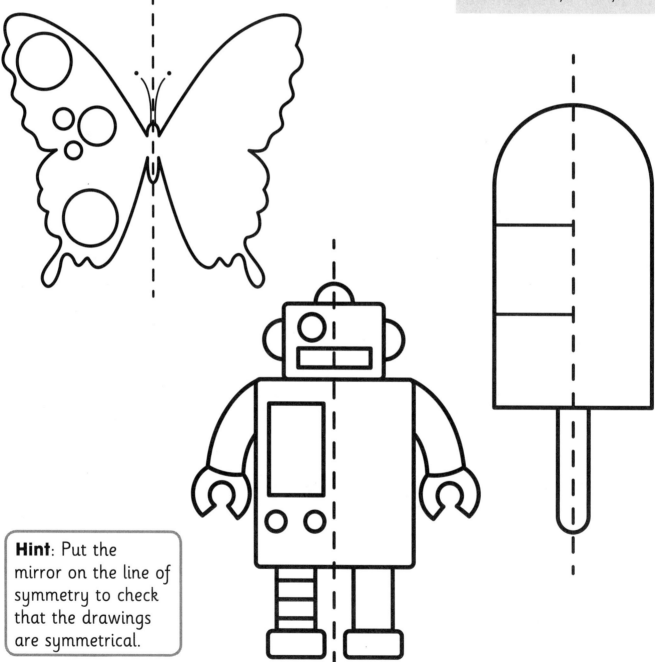

Hint: Put the mirror on the line of symmetry to check that the drawings are symmetrical.

Unit 1B Geometry and problem solving
CPM Framework 1Gs3; CPM Teacher's Resource 6.3

Tens and ones

You will need: a number line marked in tens or resource 4, page 55

Remember
Two digit numbers are made up of tens and ones.

Write how many tens.

Write the number.

Hint: Use a number line or 100 square to help count in tens and find the missing numbers.

Vocabulary
tens, ones, digit, 100 square

 10 pencils

5	tens,	50
	tens,	
	tens,	
	tens,	
	tens,	
	tens,	
	tens,	
	tens,	

Which two tens numbers are missing?

	and	

Find the secret number

Remember
Tens numbers have zero in the ones place.

You will need: a number line marked in tens or resource 4, page 55

Count in tens to find the tens number between the other two numbers. Write the tens number in the box.

Vocabulary
tens, ones, digit, 100 square

Cross out the same numbers on the balloons.
The secret number is on the balloon that is left.

It is not 80, 90, | 100 |.

It is not 40, | |, 60.

It is not 0, | |, 20.

It is not 70, | |, 90.

It is not 20, | |, 40.

It is not 80, | |, 100.

It is not 10, | |, 30.

It is not 30, | |, 50.

It is not 60, | |, 80.

The secret number is | |.

Hint: Use a number line or 100 square to support counting in tens.

Unit 1A Number and problem solving
CPM Framework 1Nn4, 1Nn8, 1Pt2, 1Pt8; CPM Teacher's Resource 7.2

11 to 20 again

You will need: resource 5, pages 56–7

Remember
Two-digit numbers are made up of tens and ones.

Vocabulary
tens, ones, place value

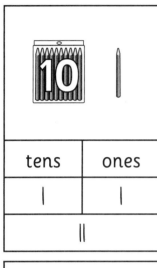

tens	ones
I	I
II	

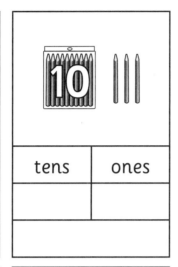

tens	ones

Write how many tens and how many ones.

Write the number.

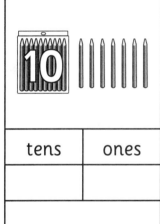

tens	ones

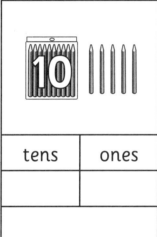

tens	ones

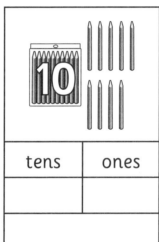

tens	ones

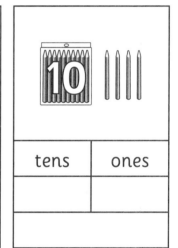

tens	ones

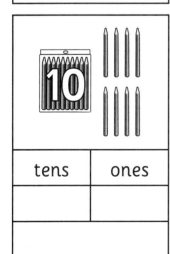

tens	ones

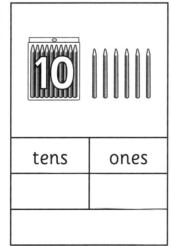

tens	ones

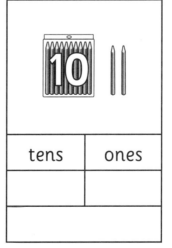

tens	ones

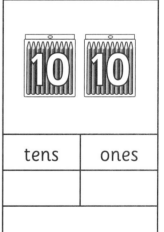

tens	ones

Hint: Use the place-value cards to find out how to write the whole number.

In my hand

You will need:
saucepan, egg cup, shoe, beaker, cubes, balls, pencils

How many can you hold in your hand?

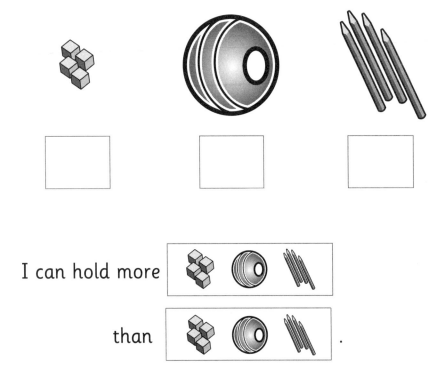

I can hold more

than

Vocabulary
estimate, hold, compare, empty, full, estimate

holds most

holds least

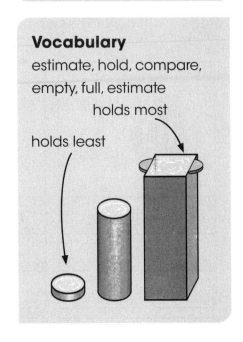

Estimate how many cubes you will need to fill each object. Then fill each object and count the cubes.

Hint: Put the cubes into tens to count them.

Items	My estimate	Number of cubes

Items	My estimate	Number of cubes

Draw a ring around the object that held the most cubes.

Unit 1C Measure and problem solving
CPM Framework 1Dh1, 1Nn1, 1Nn2, 1Nn11, 1MI2, 1MI3, 1Nn11; CPM Teacher's Resource 8.1, 8.2

Light or heavy

You will need: objects from around the room

Remember
Heavier objects press down more than lighter objects.

Vocabulary
weigh, weighs, heavy, light

Find three objects that are **lighter than a book.**
Find three objects that are **heavier than a book.**

Draw them in the table.

Hint: Use the same book each time.

heavier   lighter

lighter than 📖	heavier than 📖

Hickory, dickory, dock

Hickory, dickory, dock.
The mouse ran up the clock.
The clock struck one,
The mouse ran down,
Hickory, dickory, dock.

Hickory, dickory, dock.
The mouse ran up the clock.
The clock struck two,
The mouse lost a shoe,
Hickory, dickory, dock.

Hickory, dickory, dock.
The mouse ran up the clock.
The clock struck three,
The mouse climbed a tree,
Hickory, dickory, dock.

Hickory, dickory, dock.
The mouse ran up the clock.
The clock struck four,
He ran out of the door,
Hickory, dickory, dock.

Hickory, dickory, dock.
The mouse ran up the clock.
The clock struck five,
Look, bees from the hive!
Hickory, dickory, dock.

Hickory, dickory, dock.
The mouse ran up the clock.
The clock struck six,
Oh fiddle-sticks!
Hickory, dickory, dock.

Join in with the rhyme.

Circle the clock that matches the verse.

Hint:
Move the hands on the clock to show the time in the rhyme.

Unit 1C Measure and problem solving
CPM Framework 1Nn1, 1Nn2, 1Mt2; CPM Teacher's Resource 9.3, 9.4

Hickory, dickory, dock.
The mouse ran up the clock.
The clock struck seven,
The cat tried to get him,
Hickory, dickory, dock.

Hickory, dickory, dock.
The mouse ran up the clock.
The clock struck eight,
He's going to be late,
Hickory, dickory, dock.

Hickory, dickory, dock.
The mouse ran up the clock.
The clock struck nine,
The time's just fine,
Hickory, dickory, dock.

Hickory, dickory, dock.
The mouse ran up the clock.
The clock struck ten,
Again and again!
Hickory, dickory, dock.

Hickory, dickory, dock.
The mouse ran up the clock.
The clock struck eleven,
Four more than seven,
Hickory, dickory, dock.

Hickory, dickory, dock.
The mouse ran up the clock.
The clock struck noon,
We'll be home soon,
Hickory, dickory, dock.

Follow the path

You will need: a number line or track

Remember

Even numbers are made up of pairs. An odd number is 1 more or 1 less than an even number.

Colour the path of even numbers to get to the cheese.

Hint: Start at 0 on the number line or track. Jump on two spaces to find the next even number.

Vocabulary

pair

even numbers

odd numbers

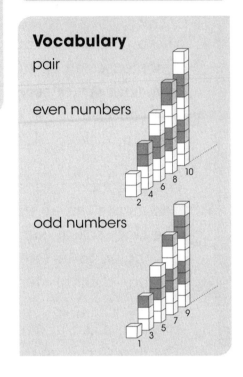

Start 0	1	7	13	15
2	3	10	12	14
4	6	8	9	16
5	17	11	5	18
13	15	19	13	20 Finish

Unit 1A Number and problem solving
CPM Framework 1Nn2, 1Nn5, 1Pt2, 1Pt7; CPM Teacher's Resource 11.1, 11.2

Odd or even?

You will need: cubes or counters

Look at the number on the card.

Pick up the same number of cubes.

Put the cubes into twos. Is the number odd or even?

Circle the correct word.

7	12	15
odd even	odd even	odd even

17	20	8
odd even	odd even	odd even

Hint: If there is a cube left over, the number must be odd.

Unit 1A Number and problem solving
CPM Framework 1Nc7, 1Nn2, 1Nn5, 1Nn7, 1Pt2 , 1Pt7; CPM Teacher's Resource 11.1, 11.2

23

Positions

You will need:
a number track

Remember
Ordinal numbers tell you the position.

Vocabulary
ordering, 1st, first, 2nd, second …

Hint: Use a number track to help with counting and ordering.

Draw a ring around the 2nd horse.

Draw a ring around the 3rd bird.

Draw a ring around the 5th fish.

Draw a ring around the 4th chicken.

Draw a ring around the 6th elephant.

Unit 1A Number and problem solving
CPM Framework 1Nn1, 1Nn2, 1Nn9; CPM Teacher's Resource 12.1

Queue for the waterhole

Hint: Use a number track to help with counting and ordering.

You will need:
a number track

Vocabulary
ordering, between, 1st, first, 2nd, second …

Where is the 🐘 in the queue? ☐

Who is between the 🦓 and the 🐊 ?

Where is the 🐊 in the queue? ☐

Who is between the 🐒 and the 🦓 ?

Where is the 🐒 in the queue? ☐

Who is between the 🦁 and the 🐘 ?

Where is the 🦜 in the queue? ☐

Add

Vocabulary
add, addition, altogether

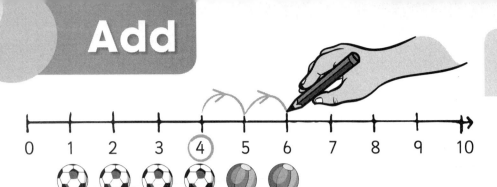

4 and 2 make 6.

4 + 2 = 6

Hint: Draw the jumps on the number line to find out how many altogether.

5 and 3 make ☐ .

5 + 3 = ☐

6 and 4 make ☐ .

6 + ☐ = ☐

8 and 5 make ☐ .

8 + ☐ = ☐

12 and ☐ make ☐ .

12 + ☐ = ☐

☐ and ☐ make ☐ .

☐ + ☐ = ☐

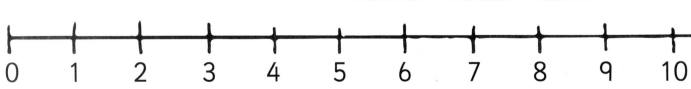

Unit 2A Number and problem solving
CPM Framework 1Nn1, 1Nn2, 1Nn3, 1Nc11, 1Nc14, 1Pt1, 1Pt2; CPM Teacher's Resource 13.2

Take away

Vocabulary
take away, less, altogether

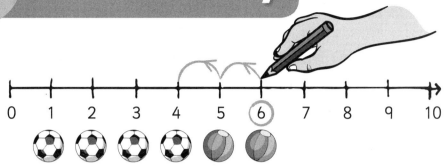

6 take away 2 is 4.

$6 - 2 = 4$

Hint: Draw the jumps on the **number line** to find out how many altogether.

If the bird eats 3 worms how many are left?

$8 - 3 = 5$

If 5 eggs are broken, how many are left?

12 EGGS

$12 - 5 = \boxed{}$

If 2 flowers die, how many are left?

$6 - \boxed{} = \boxed{}$

If 4 birds fly away, how many are left?

$10 - \boxed{} = \boxed{}$

If 3 lollipops are eaten, how many are left?

$\boxed{} - \boxed{} = \boxed{}$

Unit 2A Number and problem solving
CPM Framework 1Nn1, 1Nn2, 1Nn3, 1Nc9, 1Nc14, 1Pt1, 1Pt2; CPM Teacher's Resource 13.3, 13.4

27

Jungle track

This is game for two players. Take turns to spin the spinner. Add 2 to the spinner number. Move on that number of spaces. If you land on a shaded stone, miss your next turn. Who gets home first?

Unit 2A Number and problem solving
CPM Framework 1Nn1, 1Nn2, 1Nc8, 1Nc11, 1Nc12, 1Pt1; CPM Teacher's Resource 13.2, 13.5

You will need: two different coloured counters or coins, a pencil and paperclip to use the spinner

Hint: Use cubes, counters or a number line to add 2.

Unit 2A Number and problem solving
CPM Framework 1Nn1, 1Nn2, 1Nc8, 1Nc11, 1Nc12, 1Pt1; CPM Teacher's Resource 13.2, 13.5

Numbers to 50

Remember
Two-digit numbers are made up of tens and ones.

Vocabulary
tens, ones, place value

Write how many tens and how many ones.

Write the number.

Hint: Use place-value cards to find out how to write the whole number.

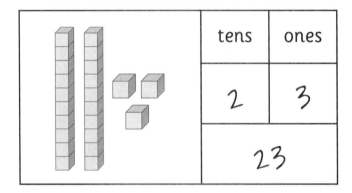

tens	ones
2	3
23	

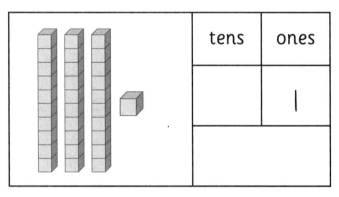

tens	ones
	1

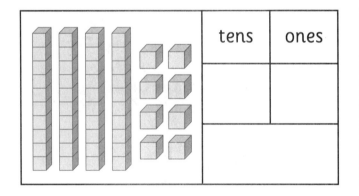

tens	ones

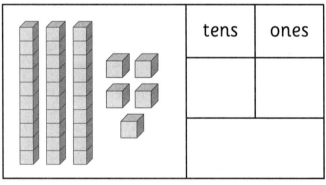

tens	ones

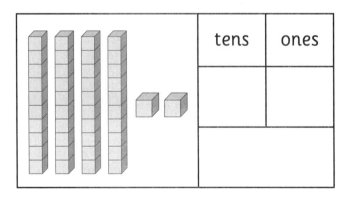

tens	ones

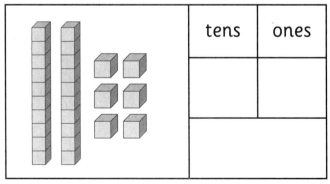

tens	ones

Unit 2A Number and problem solving
CPM Framework 1Nn6; CPM Teacher's Resource 14.1

Ordering numbers

You will need:
resource 5, pages
56–7 or a
hundred square

Vocabulary
order, ordering

1 Colour the frog with the smaller number.

a

13   17

b

16   25

c

21   12

2 Colour the flower with the larger number.

a

18   22

b

19   9

c

12   21

Hint: Look at the tens digit first to find the smaller number. Only look at the ones digit if both numbers have the same tens digit.

Shopping

Remember
You need money to buy objects.

You will need: dollars and cents or local currency or resource 6, page 58

Vocabulary
money, price, cost, buy, how much, coin, amount

Draw the coins below the objects.

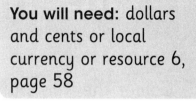

Hint: You can use dollars and cents or your local currency.

Unit 2C Measure and problem solving
CPM Framework 1Nc3, 1Nc8, 1Mm1; CPM Teacher's Resource 15.1, 15.2

How tall?

Remember
You measure height and length in the same way. Line up objects at the same starting point to compare them.

You will need: 2 centimetre interlocking cubes (or you could use the squares on resource 2, page 53), colouring pencils

Use cubes to measure the height of each character.

Who is taller than the girl? Colour their feet.

Who is shorter than the rabbit? Colour their ears.

Hint: Start from the bottom of the character and place cubes along the full height.

cubes   cubes   cubes   cubes

Full or empty?

Remember
When a container is empty, there is none left.
When a container is full, you cannot get any more in.

Vocabulary
full, empty, nearly full, nearly empty

Draw a line from each container to the matching label.

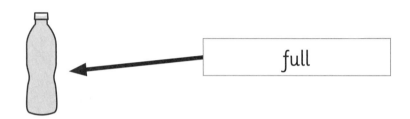

full

empty

nearly full

nearly empty

Hint: Pour a little out of a full container to make it nearly full. Add a little to an empty container to make it nearly empty.

Unit 2C Measure and problem solving
CPM Framework 1MI2; CPM Teacher's Resource 16.1

Holiday week

Join in with the rhyme.

Travel on Monday,

Arrive on Tuesday,

Play on Wednesday,

Visit on Thursday,

Relax on Friday,

Leave on Saturday,

Home on Sunday,

And that was the end

Of my holiday week!

Say what day it is today.

Now say the days in order. Start with today.

Hint: Use the rhyme to order the days of the week.

Count and sort

Remember

Count how many of each type of animal to check you have coloured the correct number of squares.

Vocabulary

count, more, less, fewer, sort, group, block graph

Look at the picture. Colour one square for each animal. Start from the bottom.

Make sure you colour the correct column.

Cross out each animal after you add it to the block graph.

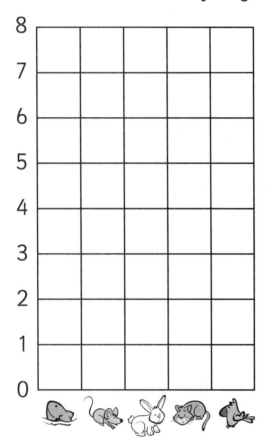

How many?

Hint: Talk about how many there are of each animal and use the words **more** and **less** (**fewer**) to compare.

Unit 2B Handling data and problem solving
CPM Framework 1Nn1, 1Nn2, 1Nn3, 1Dh1; CPM Teacher's Resource 19.1, 19.2

Number line race

You will need: two different coloured counters, a pencil and paperclip to use the spinner

Remember
Tens numbers have zeros in the ones space.

Vocabulary
ordering, tens, number, zero

This is a game for two players.

Place your counter on 50. Take turns to spin the spinner. Move your counter forwards or backwards along the number track.

The first player to reach 0 or 100 is the winner.

Play five times. Who wins more games?

0	10	20	30	40	50	60	70	80	90	100

Game	Winner
1	
2	
3	
4	
5	

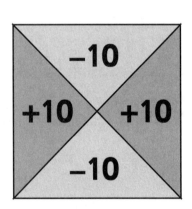

Hint: For +10 move one space towards 100.
For −10 move one space towards 0.

Unit 3A Number and problem solving
CPM Framework 1Nn7, 1Nc13, 1Pt7; CPM Teacher's Resource 20.1, 20.2

Escape the 100 square!

This is a game for two players.

Place your counter on 45, 46, 55 or 56. Take turns to spin the spinner and move your counter. The first player to move off the 100 square is the winner.

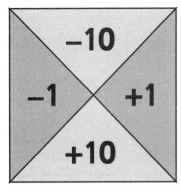

Hint: Use this picture to find out which direction to move.

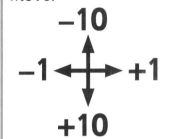

You will need: two different coloured counters, pencil and paperclip to use the spinner

1	2	3	4	5	6	7	8	9	10
11	12	13	14	15	16	17	18	19	20
21	22	23	24	25	26	27	28	29	30
31	32	33	34	35	36	37	38	39	40
41	42	43	44	45	46	47	48	49	50
51	52	53	54	55	56	57	58	59	60
61	62	63	64	65	66	67	68	69	70
71	72	73	74	75	76	77	78	79	80
81	82	83	84	85	86	87	88	89	90
91	92	93	94	95	96	97	98	99	100

Make the scales balance

Remember

The scales will only balance if the totals on each side are equal.

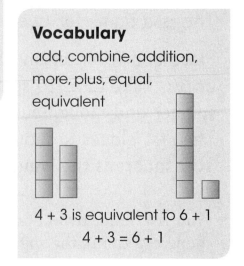

4 + 3 is equivalent to 6 + 1

$$4 + 3 = 6 + 1$$

Hint: Use the number line to find another addition to make the scales balance.

Write the numbers to make the scales balance.

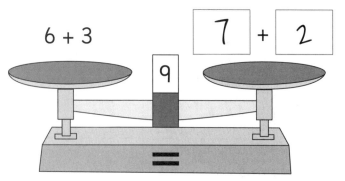

6 + 3 $\boxed{7}$ + $\boxed{2}$

9

The scales balance.

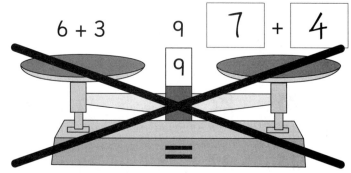

6 + 3   9 $\boxed{7}$ + $\boxed{4}$

9

The scales will not balance.

5 + 5 $\boxed{}$ + $\boxed{}$

10

7 + 5 $\boxed{}$ + $\boxed{}$

12

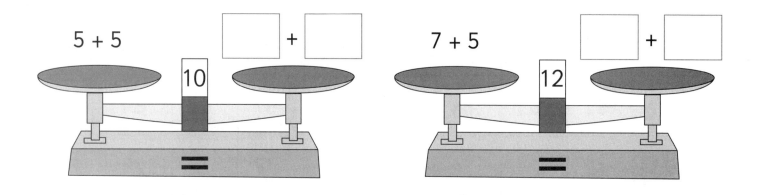

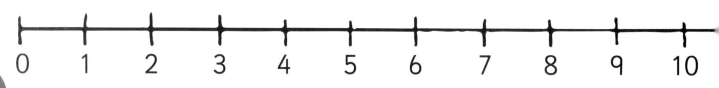

0   1   2   3   4   5   6   7   8   9   10

Unit 3A Number and problem solving
CPM Framework 1Nn10, 1Nc8, 1Nc11, 1Nc14, 1Nc17, 1Nc18, 1Pt2; CPM Teacher's Resource 21.4

8 + 0   ☐ + ☐

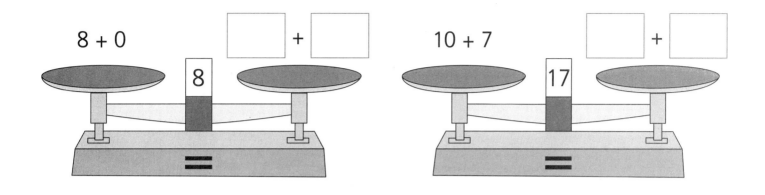

10 + 7   ☐ + ☐

☐ + ☐   6 + 7

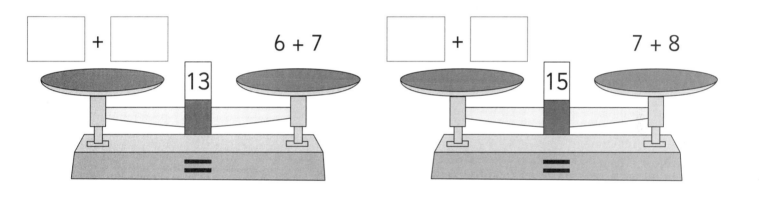

☐ + ☐   7 + 8

☐ + ☐   9 + 2

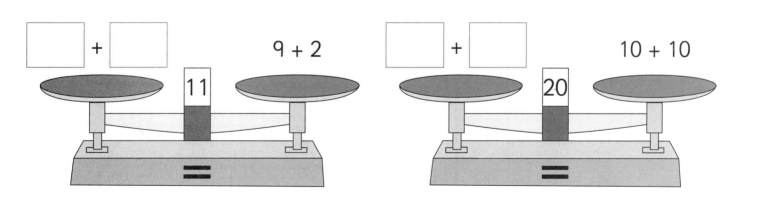

☐ + ☐   10 + 10

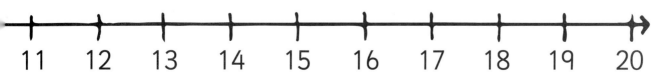

11 12 13 14 15 16 17 18 19 20

Unit 3A Number and problem solving
CPM Framework 1Nn10, 1Nc8, 1Nc11, 1Nc14, 1Nc17, 1Nc18, 1Pt2; CPM Teacher's Resource 21.4

41

Is it half?

Remember
When you halve a shape or object you have two equal pieces.

You will need: paper shapes cut from resource 3, page 54, scissors

Vocabulary
half, halves, whole

Tick the shapes that show halves.

Cross out the shapes that do not show halves.

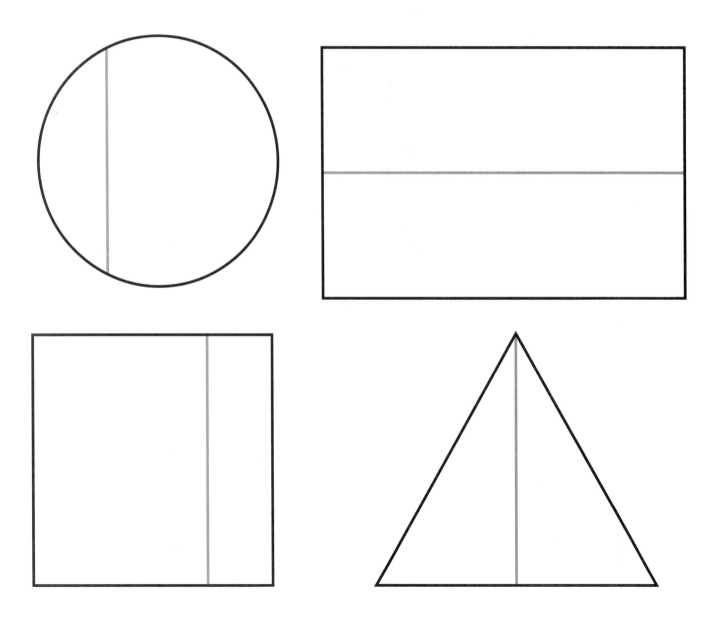

Hint: Fold cut-out shapes in half (two equal pieces) to check.

Unit 3A Number and problem solving
CPM Framework 1Nn12; CPM Teacher's Resource 22.3

Bears' fair shares

You will need: counters or cubes

Remember

When you share equally between two, both sets have the same amount.

Vocabulary

share, fair, equally

The bears share the food and drink fairly.

How many for each bear?

Each bear must have the same amount.

Hint: Use cubes to show how to share fairly.

10 spots

Remember
Number bonds for 10 help you to add to 10.

You will need: resource 7, page 59, a pencil and paperclip to use the spinner

This is a game for two players.

Take turns to spin the spinner. Draw that many spots in one of the boxes on the grid. If you cannot go, miss that turn.

Do not split up the spots. A box is full when it contains 10 spots.

The person who completes the last box wins.

Vocabulary
add, adding, addition, total, number sentence, more

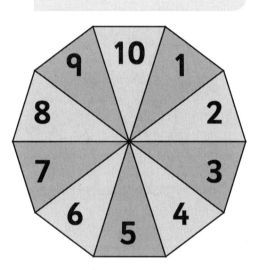

Hint: Use the 10 ant to check how many spots make 10.

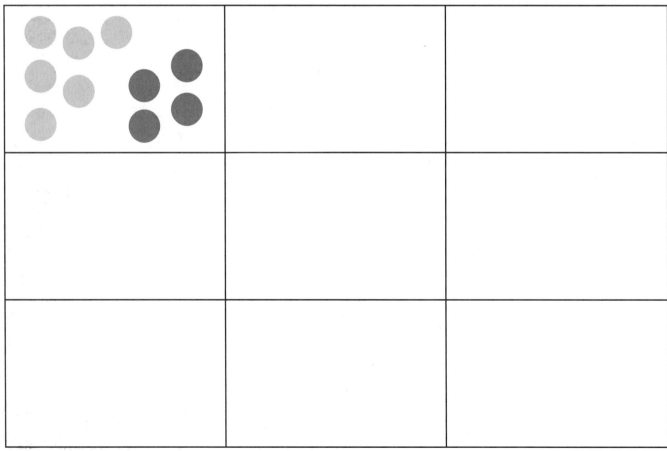

Unit 3A Number and problem solving
CPM Framework 1Nc1, 1Nc3, 1Pt1, 1Pt2; CPM Teacher's Resource 23.1

Near 10

You will need: resource 7, page 59

Vocabulary
near, add, adding, addition, total, number sentence, make

When the numbers on each pair of bags are added together, they make a near 10. Work out which number should be on the other bag.

 +  = 9

 +  = 11

 +  = 11

 +  = 9

 +  = 11

+ 3 = 11

Hint: Use the 10 ant to check the number bonds (or pairs) for 10.

Unit 3A Number and problem solving
CPM Framework 1Nn2, 1Nc2, 1Nc4, 1Nc17, 1Pt1, 1Pt2; CPM Teacher's Resource 23.1, 23.3

45

Money shells

Remember
You can add money the same way you add numbers.

You will need: four coins in each denomination of 10, 5, 2 and 1 cents or local currency or resource 6, page 58, a pencil and paperclip to use the spinner

This is a game for two players.

Place two of each of the four coins 1c, 2c, 5c, 10c, on each animal. Take turns to spin the spinner and move the matching coin from the other animal to yours. The first player to get all the coins is the winner.

How much money has the winner collected?

Vocabulary
worth, money, cent (or names of local currency), coin, total

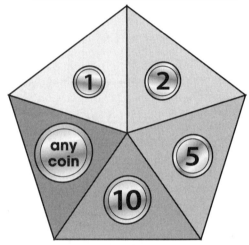

To vary the game, include a higher value coin to be taken when the spinner lands on the 'any coin' section.

Hint: Put the coins into groups worth 10c to find the total.

Unit 3C Measure and problem solving
CPM Framework 1Nc3, 1Nc11, 1Nc18, 1Mm1, 1Pt1, 1Pt2; CPM Teacher's Resource 24.1

Longer or shorter?

You will need: strips of patterned paper (or resource 8, page 60), a pencil and paperclip to use the spinner

Remember
Line up objects at the same starting point to compare them.

Take turns to spin the spinner and choose a paper strip that matches the pattern on the spinner.

If there is no matching strip, miss a turn.

When all the strips have been claimed, each player places their strips end to end in one long line.

The winner is the player with the longer line.

Vocabulary
long, longer, short, shorter

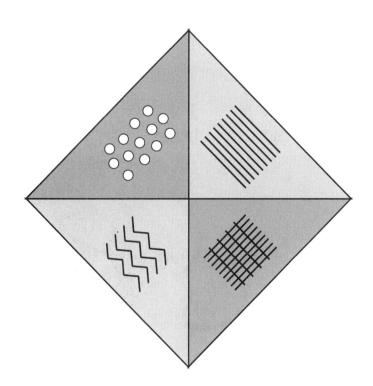

Hint: Do not leave any spaces between the strips when comparing lengths.

Comparing capacities

Remember
A larger container holds more than a smaller one.

Vocabulary
more, less, compare, holds
more, holds less, capacity

Draw a line to put each container in the correct order in the boxes.

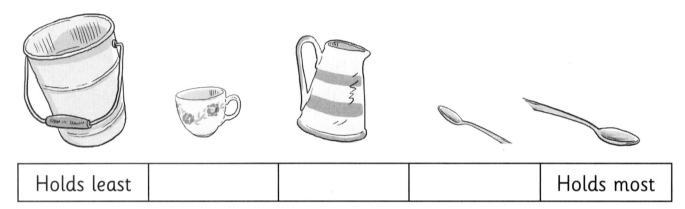

Holds least				Holds most

Ring **more** or **less** in each box to make the sentence true.

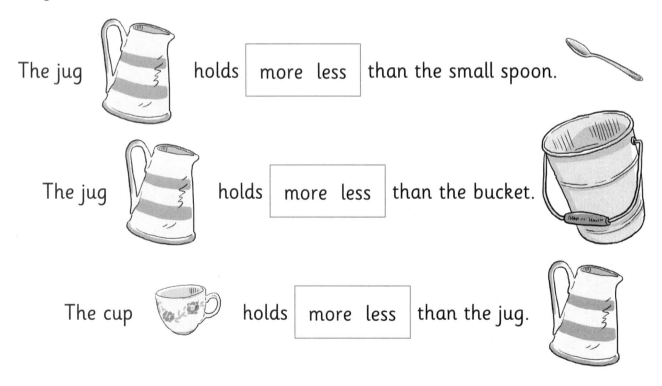

The jug holds [more less] than the small spoon.

The jug holds [more less] than the bucket.

The cup holds [more less] than the jug.

The cup holds [more less] than the big spoon.

Unit 3C Measure and problem solving
CPM Framework 1MI2, 1MI3; CPM Teacher's Resource 26.1, 26.2

What time is it?

You will need: a clock with movable hands (You could make a clock from a paper plate, a split pin and two cardboard hands.)

Remember
The minute hand is the long hand. It points to the 12 for an o'clock time. The hour hand is the short hand. It points to the hour number.

Vocabulary
clock, hands, hour, minute, hour hand, minute hand, o'clock

Write the time.

_____ o'clock

_____ o'clock

_____ o'clock

_____ o'clock

Which number does the minute hand point to at every o'clock time?

_____

Draw the minute hand on the clock.

Hint: Move the hands on the clock to show the matching time.

Field mice

Remember
Data can be collected and shown in different ways.

Hint: Tick the mice as you count them.

Count the mice to find out how many there are in each field.

How many mice altogether? ☐ mice.

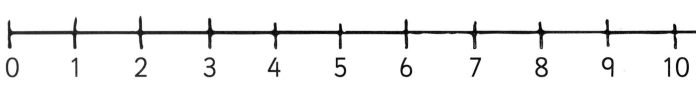

Unit 3B Handling data and problem solving
CPM Framework 1Nn2, 1Nn3, 1Dh1, 1Pt1, 1Pt2; CPM Teacher's Resource 28.1, 28.3

Write the correct number of mice in each field.

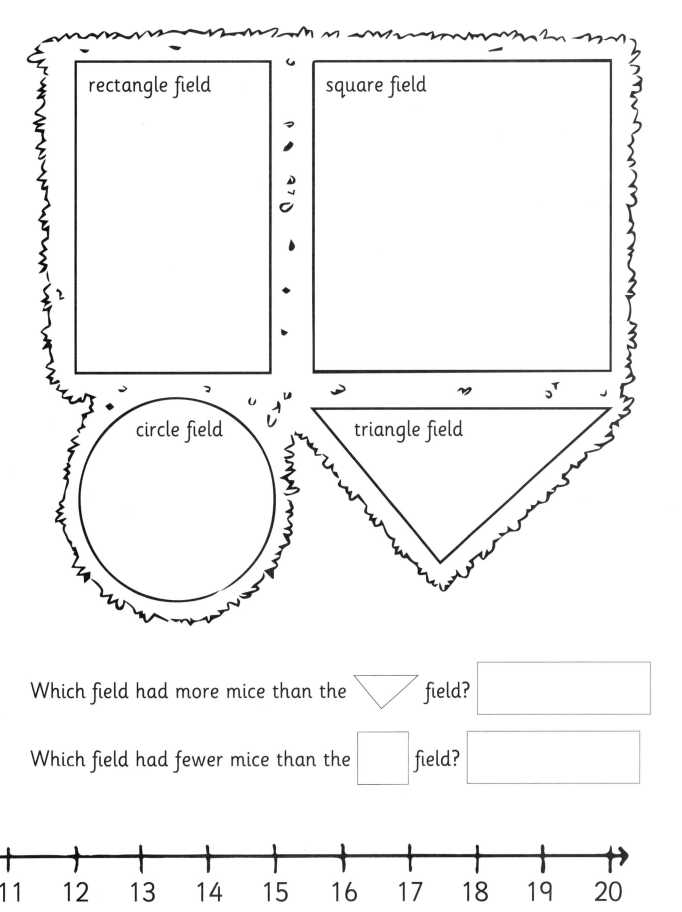

rectangle field

square field

circle field

triangle field

Which field had more mice than the ▽ field?

Which field had fewer mice than the ☐ field?

11 12 13 14 15 16 17 18 19 20

Unit 3B Handling data and problem solving
CPM Framework 1Nn2, 1Nn3, 1Dh1, 1Pt1, 1Pt2; CPM Teacher's Resource 28.1, 28.3

51

Ingredients

$\frac{1}{2}$ cup of salt

$\frac{1}{2}$ cup of water

1 cup of flour

How to make the salt dough

Mix the salt into the flour in a bowl.

Gradually add the water, stirring it into the flour and salt mixture.

Stop adding water when you have a fairly dry dough.

If the dough is sticky add more flour.

Knead the dough thoroughly.

It is now ready for use.

Shapes made from the dough can be dried in an oven, at low heat, for about three hours.

Dried shapes may be painted.

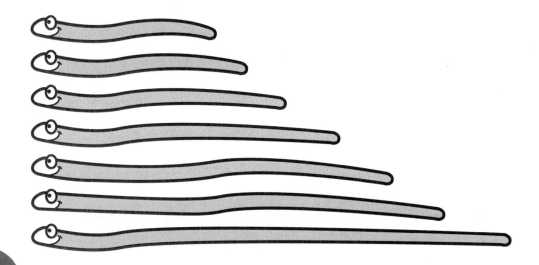

Resource 2 Square measures

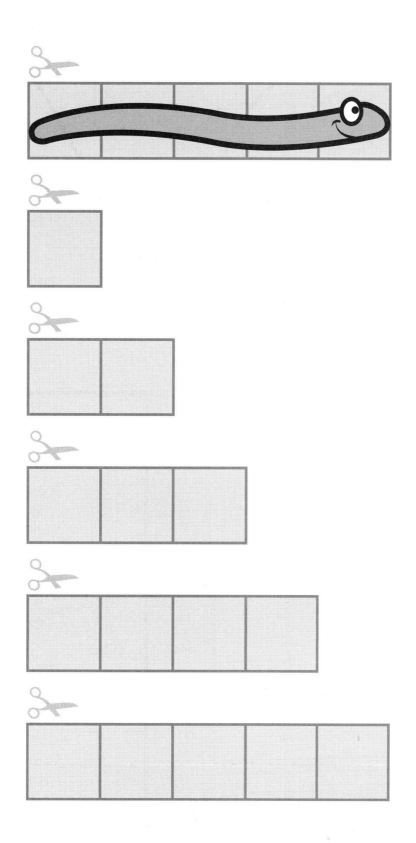

Resource 3 Shapes

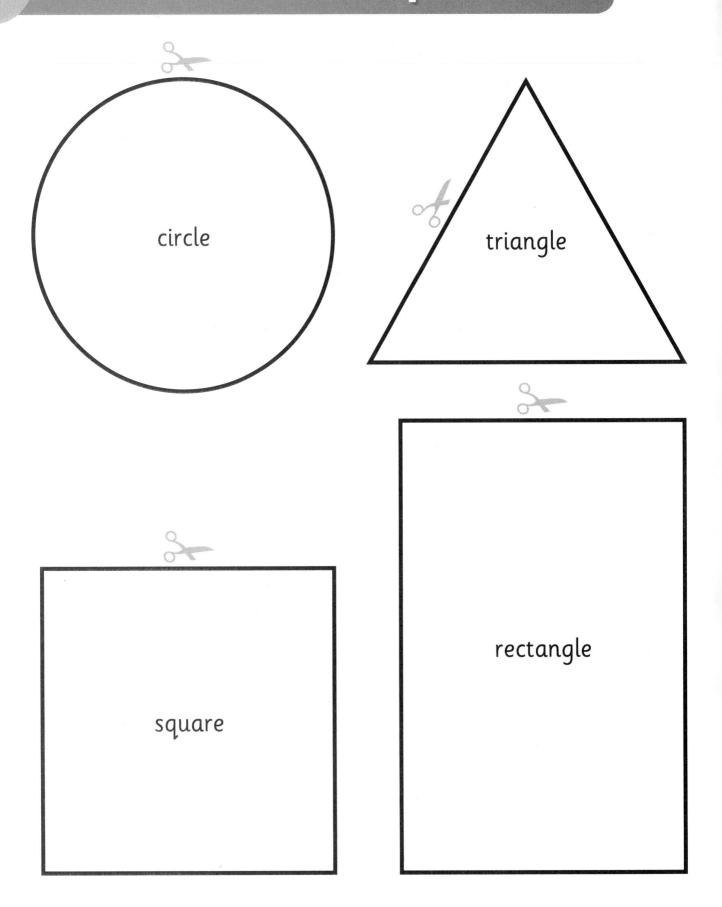

circle

triangle

square

rectangle

Photocopiable resources

Number line

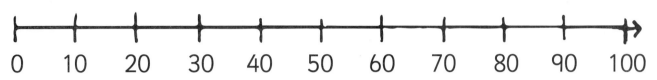

0   10   20   30   40   50   60   70   80   90   100

100 square

1	2	3	4	5	6	7	8	9	10
11	12	13	14	15	16	17	18	19	20
21	22	23	24	25	26	27	28	29	30
31	32	33	34	35	36	37	38	39	40
41	42	43	44	45	46	47	48	49	50
51	52	53	54	55	56	57	58	59	60
61	62	63	64	65	66	67	68	69	70
71	72	73	74	75	76	77	78	79	80
81	82	83	84	85	86	87	88	89	90
91	92	93	94	95	96	97	98	99	100

1	0	0	
1	0		1
2	0		2
3	0		3
4	0		4

5	0		ϛ
6	0		9
7	0		ㄥ
8	0		8
9	0		b

Photocopiable resources

10 ant

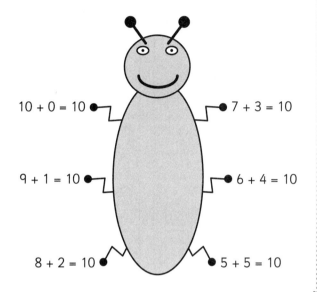

10 + 0 = 10
7 + 3 = 10
9 + 1 = 10
6 + 4 = 10
8 + 2 = 10
5 + 5 = 10

10 ant

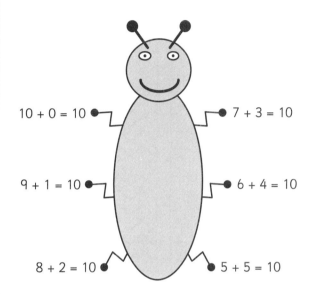

10 + 0 = 10
7 + 3 = 10
9 + 1 = 10
6 + 4 = 10
8 + 2 = 10
5 + 5 = 10

10 ant

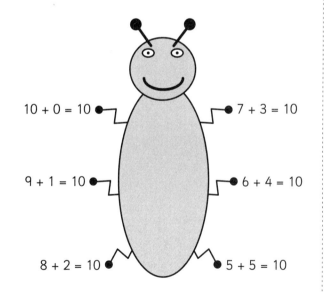

10 + 0 = 10
7 + 3 = 10
9 + 1 = 10
6 + 4 = 10
8 + 2 = 10
5 + 5 = 10

10 ant

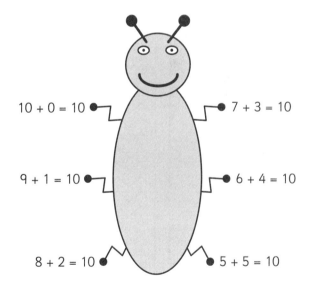

10 + 0 = 10
7 + 3 = 10
9 + 1 = 10
6 + 4 = 10
8 + 2 = 10
5 + 5 = 10

Resource 8 Patterned strips

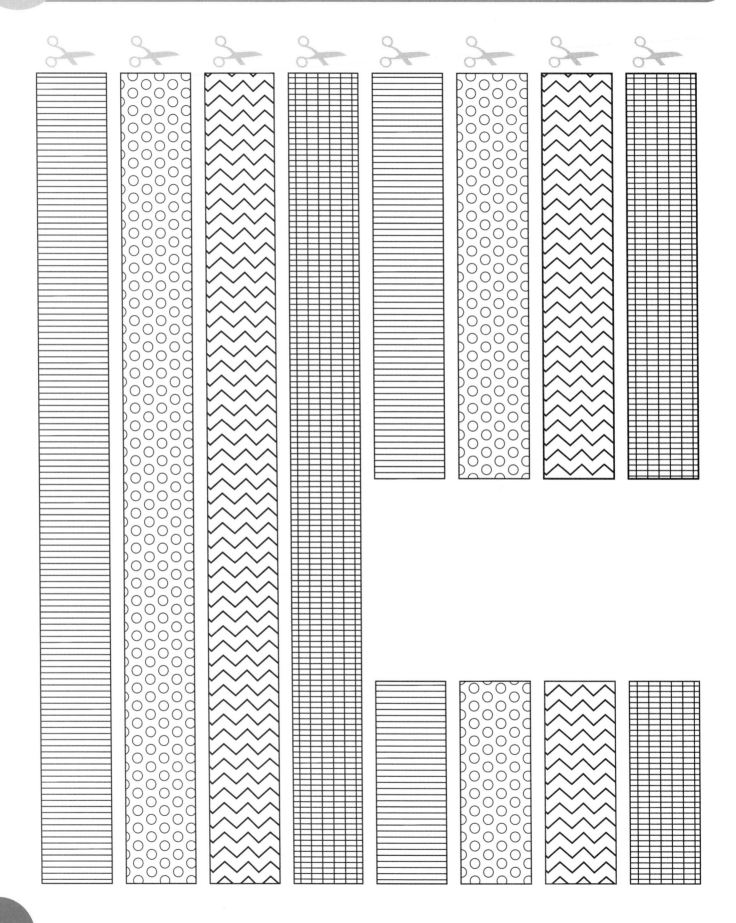

Answers

Page 4 Toy cupboard

7 balls, 9 books, 5 teddy bears, 6 dolls, 4 robots, 10 toy cars, 8 crayons/coloured pencils.

Page 5 Make 10

2 + 8 = 10
3 + 7 = 10
4 + 6 = 10
5 + 5 = 10
10 + 0 = 10.

Page 6 Dough worms

Children's own answers.

Page 7 Cube worms

Children's own answers.

Pages 8–9 Numbers 11 to 20

10 and 2 make 12.
10 and 3 make 13.
10 and 4 make 14.
10 and 5 make 15.
10 and 6 make 16.
10 and 7 make 17.
10 and 8 make 18.
10 and 9 make 19.
10 and 10 make 20.

Page 10 Estimating

7

15

9

18

Page 11 More estimating

	Fewer than 10	✓	More than 10	
	Count		3	
	Fewer than 10		More than 10	✓
	Count		19	
	Fewer than 10	✓	More than 10	
	Count		8	
	Fewer than 10		More than 10	✓
	Count		12	
	Fewer than 10	✓	More than 10	
	Count		7	

Page 12 What's left?

The rectangles are left.

Page 13 3D shape builder

Children's own models.

Page 14 Symmetry

Children's own drawings.

Page 15 Tens and ones

Row 2: 2 tens, 20.
Row 3: 8 tens, 80.
Row 4: 6 tens, 60.
Row 5: 3 tens, 30.
Row 6: 7 tens, 70.
Row 7: 10 tens, 100.
Row 8: 1 ten, 10.
40 and 90 are missing.

Page 16 Find the secret number

It is not 40, 50, 60.
It is not 0, 10, 20.
It is not 70, 80, 90.
It is not 20, 30 , 40.
It is not 80, 90, 100.
It is not 10, 20, 30.
It is not 30, 40, 50.
It is not 60, 70, 80.
The secret number is 60.

Page 17 11 to 20 again

13; 17, 15, 19, 14, 18, 16, 12, 20

Page 18 In my hand

Answers will depend on the size of the objects used. The object that holds the greatest number of cubes holds the most.

Page 19 Light or heavy

Heavier than a book: group table, chair, bookshelf with books on, cupboard, set of classroom drawers.
Lighter than a book: cube, sweet, balloon, feather, pencil.
Children's own drawings of heavy and light objects.

Pages 20–21 Hickory, dickory, dock

Check that children place the hands of the clock correctly to show the times, from one o'clock through to 12 o'clock (noon).

Page 22 Follow the path

Start 0	1	7	13	15
2	3	10	12	14
4	6	8	9	16
5	17	11	5	18
13	15	19	13	20 Finish

Page 23 Odd or even?

7 odd, 12 even, 15 odd, 17 odd, 20 even, 8 even.

Page 24 Positions

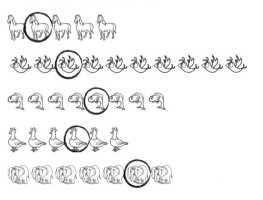

Page 25 Queue for the waterhole

Elephant is 6th.
Giraffe is between zebra and crocodile.
Crocodile is 3rd.
Elephant is between monkey and zebra.
Monkey is 7th.
Monkey is between lion and elephant.
Parrot is 1st.

Page 26 Add

5 and 3 make 8, 5 + 3 = 8.
6 and 4 make 10, 6 + 4 = 10.
8 and 5 make 13, 8 + 5 = 13.
12 and 3 make 15, 12 + 3 = 15.
10 and 7 make 17, 10 + 7 = 17.

Page 27 Take away

12 − 5 = 7.
6 − 2 = 4.
10 − 4 = 6.
15 − 3 = 12.

Pages 28–29 Jungle track

Game – no answers.

Page 30 Numbers to 50

Box 2: 31, box 3: 48, box 4: 35, box 5: 42, box 6: 26.

Page 31 Ordering numbers

1a

1b

1c

2a

2b

2c

Page 32 Shopping

Children's choice of use of coins.

Page 33 How tall?

King: 8 cubes tall, mouse: 2 cubes tall, girl: 3 cubes tall, rabbit: 5 cubes tall.
The king and the rabbit are taller than the girl.
The girl and the mouse are shorter than the rabbit.

Page 34 Full or empty?

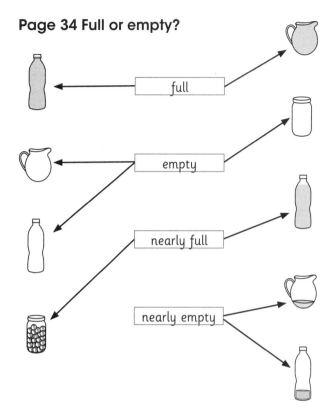

Page 35 Holiday week

None.

Pages 36–37 Count and sort

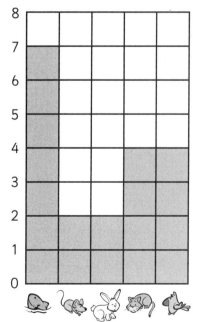

Page 38 Number line race

Game – no answers.

Page 39 Escape the 100 square!

Game – no answers.

Pages 40–41 Make the scales balance

Children's own answers.

Page 42 Is it half?

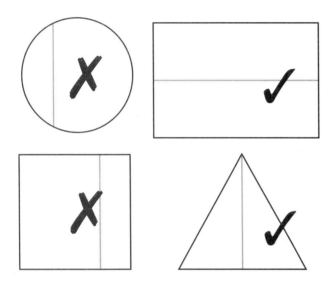

Page 43 Bears' fair shares

1	2	5	2	3	1

Page 44 10 spots

Game – no answers.

Page 45 Near 10

Set 2: 9 + 2 = 11.
Set 3: 7 + 4 = 11.
Set 4: 5 + 4 = 9.
Set 5: 6 + 5 = 11.
Set 6: 8 + 3 = 11.

Page 46 Money shells

Total of all coins = 72c (or local currency).

Page 47 Longer or shorter?

Game – no answers.

Page 48 Comparing capacities

The jug holds more than the small spoon.
The jug holds less than the bucket.
The cup holds less than the jug.
The cup holds more than the big spoon.

Page 49 What time is it?

11 o'clock.
1 o'clock.
3 o'clock.
10 o'clock.
12.

Page 50–51 Field mice

There are 19 mice altogether.
The rectangle field has more mice than the triangle field.
The circle field had fewer (less) mice than the square field.